Healthy Porridge Cookbook

My Wide Collection of Oatmeal-based Recipes Suiting All Kinds of Different Tastes

Simple & Easy-to-Prepare! Plus, Free Bonus Oatmeal Cookie Recipes!

BY: Nancy Silverman

COPYRIGHT NOTICES

Table of Contents

Introduction

Porridge is a meal found around the globe; it is part of many cultures' daily meal menus. People from various cultures or walks of life have a passion for porridge. All have different preferences of serving, such as watery, thick, salty, hot, or cold. Porridge is a versatile dish that can be served in many different ways; thirty of my personal favourites are here within these pages that I am happy to share with you! Try using my porridge recipes as a kind of base or guide towards helping you create your particular type of porridge that suits your tastes! Do not be afraid to add to the ingredients and make your extra porridge special! There is nothing better than enjoying a meal that not only tastes great but is very healthy too! For me, I see this combination as a win, win! So, now I say it is time for less talk and more preparing your special porridge for the day!

Collection of Porridge Recipes

Apple & Spiced Raisin Porridge

A yummy porridge recipe for those that are fond of apples!

Prep Time: 4 minutes

Cook Time: 8 minutes

Servings: 2

Instructions:

Porridge base:

- 1 teaspoon vanilla extract
- ½ cup rolled oats
- ½ cup whole milk
- ½ cup water
- maple syrup or honey to taste

Toppings:

- 3 tablespoons raisins
- 2 large chopped apples
- a dash of nutmeg powder
- a dash of cinnamon powder
- 1 squeeze of fresh lemon juice

Directions:

1. Mix all of your oat ingredients in a pot and combine well.

2. Bring oat mixture to a boil over medium heat setting, then simmer for 8 minutes or until porridge reaches your preferred consistency. Stir porridge occasionally, and remove from heat once cooked.

3. Spoon your oats into the serving bowls.

4. Add the toppings to a bowl and mix. Add your topping mixture to your porridge and serve!

Grilled Fig & Ginger Porridge

A yummy treat of fresh figs and healthy porridge for all to enjoy!

Prep Time:3 minutes

Cook Time:9 minutes

Servings:2

Instructions:

Porridge base:

- 1 teaspoon ginger powder
- ½ cup rolled oats
- ½ cup whole milk
- ½ cup water
- maple syrup or honey to taste

Toppings:

- Chopped stem ginger in syrup
- grilled figs, sliced

Directions:

1. Combine all of your porridge ingredients in a pot and stir to mix well.

2. Bring your porridge mixture to a boil over medium heat for about 8 minutes; or until your desired consistency is reached. Remove from heat.

3. Add the porridge to serving bowls. Add your toppings and serve.

Cranberry & Cinnamon Porridge

A healthy porridge recipe that offers you a fantastic balance of tanginess and sweetness!

Prep Time: 3 minutes

Cook Time: 8 minutes

Servings:2

Instructions:

Porridge base:

- ½ tablespoon butter
- ½ cup rolled oats
- ½ cup water
- ½ cup whole milk
- 1 teaspoon vanilla extract
- maple syrup or honey to taste
- a dash of sea salt

Toppings:

- butter
- cranberry compote
- chopped nuts
- cinnamon powder

Directions:

1. Mix all of your porridge ingredients in a pot over a medium heat setting. Stir to combine well, and bring to boil. Cook for 8 minutes or until you have reached desired consistency. Remove from heat.

2. Spoon your porridge or oat mixture into serving bowls, then add toppings. Serve and enjoy!

Norwegian Berry & Cream Porridge

A recipe that may sound intimidating but is simple to prepare!

Prep Time: 3 minutes

Cook Time: 8 minutes

Servings: 2

Instructions:

Porridge base:

- 1 cup whole milk
- a dash of sea salt
- ½ cup rolled oats
- a dash of cinnamon powder

Toppings:

- Mixed berries of your choice
- fresh cream
- maple syrup

Directions:

1. Add all of your oat ingredients into a pot and mix well.

2. Bring oat mixture to a boil over medium heat, then reduce heat, allowing it to simmer for approximately 8 minutes or until desired consistency is reached. Stir occasionally, and turn the heat off.

3. Spoon the oats into serving bowls, then add toppings and serve warm.

Banana & Quinoa Oat Porridge

Enjoy this porridge recipe with its' yummy and enriching toppings!

Prep Time:3 minutes

Cook Time:9 minutes

Servings:4

Instructions:

Porridge base:

- 1 teaspoon cinnamon powder
- 1 ½ cups whole milk
- 1 teaspoon vanilla extract
- ½ cup quinoa
- ½ cup rolled oats
- brown sugar to taste

Toppings:

- toasted nuts, chopped
- ½ cup raisins
- 2 large bananas, sliced
- maple syrup as needed

Directions:

1. Combine all of your oat ingredients in a large pot and mix well to combine.

2. Bring oat mixture to a boil over medium heat setting, then reduce the heat and simmer for 9 minutes or until desired consistency of porridge is reached. Occasionally stir porridge, then remove from heat.

3. Add your porridge to serving bowls. Add your toppings to porridge and serve warm.

Avocado & Egg Porridge

Excellent light and healthy porridge recipe that will energize you!

Prep Time: 3 minutes

Cook Time: 9 minutes

Servings: 2

Instructions:

Porridge base:

- 1 cup rolled oats
- salt and pepper to taste
- 2 teaspoons tahini
- 1 ½ cups vegetable stock

Toppings:

- 4 poached eggs
- avocado slices
- sesame seeds
- Chia seeds

Directions:

1. Mix all of your ingredients for oats in a pot and stir well.

2. Bring oat mixture to a boil over medium heat setting, then reduce heat and simmer for 9 minutes or until desired consistency is reached. Stir porridge occasionally, then when done, remove from heat.

3. Add porridge to serving bowls, add toppings and serve warm.

Spinach & Tomato Porridge

Try this highly nutritious spinach and tomato porridge recipe!

Prep Time:5 minutes

Cook Time:15 minutes

Servings:4

Instructions:

- ½ cup baby spinach, chopped
- dash of red chili flakes
- ½ cup cherry tomatoes, halved
- ½ cup mushrooms, sliced
- squeeze of fresh lemon juice
- 1 cup rolled oats
- 1 garlic clove, minced
- 1 ½ cups vegetable broth
- 1 white onion, finely chopped
- 1 teaspoon olive oil

Directions:

1. Heat-up olive oil in a large pot over medium heat.

2. Add the mushrooms and onion, then sauté for 5-minutes or until tender.

3. Stir in your minced garlic and cook until fragrant.

4. Add your tomatoes and cook them for a few minutes.

5. Add your vegetable broth, oats, red chili flakes, salt and pepper. Stir mixture to combine, bring to a boil, lower heat, and simmer for 7-minutes or until porridge reaches the desired consistency.

Coffee Cake Porridge

Serve this porridge recipe with a nice soothing cup of coffee!

Prep Time: 3 minutes

Cook Time: 9 minutes

Servings: 2

Instructions:

Porridge base:

- ½ cup whole milk
- ½ cup rolled oats
- dash of cinnamon powder
- ½ teaspoon vanilla extract
- ½ cup freshly brewed coffee
- maple syrup to taste
- Toppings:
- toasted walnuts, chopped
- raisins

Directions:

1. Combine all of your oat ingredients in a large pot and mix well.

2. Bring your oat mixture to a boil over medium heat setting, then reduce heat and simmer for 8-minutes or until desired consistency is reached. Stir porridge occasionally while cooking, then remove from heat.

3. Spoon oats into serving bowls and add your toppings and serve!

Bacon & Mushroom Porridge

A tasty porridge recipe that will make for the perfect brunch that will be easy on the tummy!

Prep Time: 5 minutes

Cook Time: 16 minutes

Servings: 4

Instructions:

Porridge base:

- 1 onion, finely chopped
- 4 bacon slices, chopped
- ½ cup mushrooms, sliced
- 1 cup rolled oats
- 1 garlic clove, minced
- 1 ½ cups vegetable stock
- sea salt to taste

Toppings:

- red chili flakes as needed
- fresh parsley, chopped for garnish
- 4 eggs, sunny-side-up

Directions:

1. Heat a pot over medium heat setting and add your bacon. Cook the bacon for about 5-minutes or until golden brown.

2. Add the onion, mushrooms, garlic to the pot and sauté for about 5-minutes or until tender.

3. Pour your oats into stock and season with sea salt; stir well and bring to mixture to a boil.

4. Reduce the heat to low, then simmer for 8-minutes or until you reach desired consistency.

5. Spoon the porridge into your serving bowls, top with the eggs, and garnish with red chili flakes and parsley. Serve warm and enjoy!

Protein-Filled Porridge

Here is a healthy and tasty bowl full of protein-filled porridge!

Prep Time:3 minutes

Cook Time:11 minutes

Servings:4

Instructions:

Porridge base:

- 1 cup milk
- ½ cup rolled oats
- ½ cup quinoa
- ½ cup white lentils
- 1 teaspoon vanilla extract
- ¾ teaspoon vanilla protein powder
- dash of sea salt

Toppings:

- fruit compote of choice
- coconut flakes
- nut butter
- chopped nuts & seeds of choice

Directions:

1. Mix all of your oat ingredients in a pot and stir to combine.

2. Bring oat mixture to a boil over medium heat setting or until the porridge has reached desired consistency.

3. Add porridge to serving bowls, then add toppings. Serve warm and enjoy!

Chocolate Avocado Porridge

Each mouthful of this porridge recipe will melt in your mouth!

Prep Time: 3 minutes

Cook Time: 8 minutes

Servings: 2

Instructions:

Porridge base:

- 2 teaspoons cocoa powder,
- plus extra to use for dusting
- ½ cup rolled oats
- 1 teaspoon vanilla extract
- brown sugar to taste
- ½ cup milk
- ½ cup water

Toppings:

- cocoa nibs
- avocado slices
- cocoa powder for dusting

Directions:

1. Combine all of your oat ingredients in a pot.

2. Bring your porridge mixture to a boil over medium heat setting for 8-minutes, or until porridge reaches desired consistency.

3. Add porridge to serving bowls, then add slices of avocado and cocoa nibs.

4. Dust the top with cocoa powder and serve warm.

Coconut & Blueberry Porridge

Chocolate and coconut make a perfect combo in this porridge recipe!

Prep Time:3 minutes

Cook Time:10 minutes

Servings:2

Instructions:

Porridge base:

- ½ cup rolled oats
- maple syrup to taste
- a dash of sea salt
- ½ cup coconut milk
- ½ cup water
- 3 dates, pitted, chopped
- 2 teaspoons cocoa powder
- 1 teaspoon vanilla extract
- 1 tablespoon desiccated coconut

Toppings:

- 2 teaspoons cacao nibs
- 1 tablespoon coconut shavings
- maple syrup to taste

Directions:

1. Combine all of your oat ingredients in a pot and mix well.

2. Bring porridge mixture to a boil over a medium heat setting for 10- minutes or until the porridge is desired.

3. Add porridge to serving bowls, then add your toppings and serve warm.

Plum & Almond Porridge

Here is a fun porridge recipe that you can use to incorporate plums into your meal!

Prep Time: 3 minutes

Cook Time: 10 minutes

Servings: 2

Instructions:

Porridge base:

- 1 orange, zested & juiced
- ½ cup rolled oats
- ½ teaspoon vanilla extract
- ¼ teaspoon cinnamon powder
- ½ cup almond milk
- maple syrup to taste

Toppings:

- 6 plums, halved and stones removed
- ½ cup almonds, chopped

Directions:

1. Mix the oat ingredients into a pot.

2. Bring your pot to a boil over medium heat setting for 8-minutes or until the porridge has reached desired consistency. Stir occasionally through the cooking process.

3. Add porridge to serving bowls, then top with toppings and serve!

Pomegranate & Berries Porridge

A tasty and healthy way to spoil yourself in the morning!

Prep Time:3 minutes

Cook Time:9 minutes

Servings:2

Instructions:

Porridge base:

- ½ cup almond milk
- ½ cup rolled oats
- ½ cup water
- maple syrup to taste

Toppings:

- crushed pistachios
- fresh raspberries and blueberries
- fresh pomegranate seeds

Directions:

1. Mix all of your oat ingredients in a pot.

2. Bring your pot to a boil over medium heat setting for 9-minutes, or until porridge reaches desired consistency.

3. Spoon the porridge into serving bowls, then top with toppings. Serve warm and enjoy!

Spiced Orange Porridge

A perfect porridge recipe to serve for breakfast on a cool fall morning!

Prep Time: 3 minutes

Cook Time: 9 minutes

Servings: 2

Instructions:

Porridge base:

- 1 teaspoon fresh orange zest
- ½ cup rolled oats
- 1 tablespoon fresh orange juice
- ½ teaspoon cinnamon powder
- ½ teaspoon ginger powder
- 1 teaspoon vanilla extract
- ½ cup almond milk
- ½ cup water
- maple syrup to taste

Toppings:

- raisins
- orange slices
- sunflower seeds

Directions:

1. Mix all of your oat ingredients in a pot.

2. Bring your oat mixture to a boil over medium heat setting for about 9-minutes or until the porridge has reached desired consistency.

3. Dish the porridge out between serving bowls, then add toppings. Serve warm and enjoy!

Blueberry & Lemon Porridge

Enjoy this simple porridge recipe that will create an exciting burst of flavour in your mouth!

Prep Time: 3 minutes

Cook Time: 9 minutes

Servings: 2

Instructions:

Porridge base:

- ½ cup rolled oats
- 2 teaspoons fresh lemon zest
- ½ teaspoon cinnamon powder
- 1 teaspoon vanilla extract
- ½ cup water
- ½ cup almond milk
- 2 teaspoons light brown sugar
- a dash of sea salt

Toppings:

- fresh lemon zest
- fresh blueberries

Directions:

1. Mix all of your oat ingredients in a pot.

2. Place the pot over medium heat, setting for 9-minutes or until porridge reaches desired consistency.

3. Add porridge to your serving bowls, then top with blueberries.

4. Garnish porridge with lemon zest. Serve warm and enjoy!

Chocolate Orange Porridge

A tasty and healthy porridge recipe that your kids are sure to love!

Prep Time:3 minutes

Cook Time:9 minutes

Servings:2

Instructions:

Porridge base:

- 1 teaspoon vanilla extract
- ½ cup rolled oats
- ½ cup almond milk
- ½ cup water
- 1 teaspoon fresh orange zest
- maple syrup to taste

Toppings:

- chocolate shavings
- sweet orange sections

Directions:

1. Mix all of the oat ingredients into a pot.

2. Bring your porridge mixture to a boil over medium heat setting, then reduce to low and simmer for 8-minutes, or until porridge reaches desired consistency.

3. Add to serving bowls, then add your toppings. Serve warm and enjoy!

Tropical Mix Porridge

Try this yummy exotic tropical fruit porridge recipe that is sure to please your taste buds!

Prep Time:3 minutes

Cook Time:9 minutes

Servings:2

Instructions:

Porridge base:

- 1 teaspoon vanilla extract
- ½ cup rolled oats
- ½ teaspoon banana extract
- ½ cup almond milk
- ½ cup water
- maple syrup to taste

Toppings:

- sliced fresh bananas
- scooped passion fruit
- kiwis, peeled and sliced
- mangoes, chopped
- sliced nuts

Directions:

1. Mix all of your oat ingredients in a pot.

2. Bring porridge mixture to a boil over medium heat setting for 9-minutes or until porridge reaches desired consistency.

3. Add your porridge to serving bowls, then add the toppings. Serve warm and enjoy!

Ginger Peach Porridge

The combination of ginger and peach makes a perfect duo in this recipe!

Prep Time: 3 minutes

Cook Time: 10 minutes

Servings: 2

Instructions:

Porridge base:

- 1 teaspoon vanilla extract
- ½ cup rolled oats
- a dash of ginger paste
- ½ cup almond milk
- ½ cup water
- maple syrup to taste

Toppings:

- Sliced fresh or baked peaches

Directions:

1. Mix all of your oat ingredients in a pot.

2. Bring your pot to a boil over medium heat setting, then reduce to low heat and simmer for about 10-minutes, or until the porridge has reached desired consistency. Stir occasionally during the cooking process. Once cooked, remove from heat.

3. Add your porridge into serving bowls, then add peaches and serve warm.

Berry & Nut Butter Porridge

Enjoy this tasty porridge recipe with the merge of berries and nut butter!

Prep Time: 3 minutes

Cook Time: 10 minutes

Servings:2

Instructions:

Porridge base:

- ½ cup almond milk
- 1 teaspoon vanilla extract
- 2 tablespoons nut butter of choice
- ¼ cup fresh raspberries and blueberries
- ½ cup rolled oats
- ½ cup water
- maple syrup to taste

Toppings:

- maple syrup to taste
- fresh raspberries and blueberries
- nuts (peanuts, almonds, etc.)

Directions:

1. Mix all of your oat ingredients in a pot.

2. Bring your oat mixture to a boil over medium heat setting, then reduce heat to low and simmer for 10-minutes or until the porridge has reached desired consistency.

3. Add your porridge to your serving bowls, then top with toppings and serve warm.

Creamy Mango Porridge

If you enjoy a super creamy porridge, then I suggest you try this porridge recipe!

Prep Time: 3 minutes

Cook Time: 10 minutes

Servings: 2

Instructions:

Porridge base:

- 1 tablespoon desiccated coconut
- ½ cup rolled oats
- ½ cup almond milk
- 1 teaspoon vanilla extract
- ½ cup Greek yogurt
- a dash of sea salt
- maple syrup to taste

Toppings:

- honey to taste
- chopped mangoes
- coconut flakes

Directions:

1. Combine all of your oat ingredients in a pot.

2. Bring your pot to a boil over medium heat setting, then reduce to low heat and simmer for 10-minutes, or until the porridge has reached the desired consistency. Stir porridge occasionally through the cooking process. Once cooked, remove from heat.

3. Add your porridge to your serving bowls, then add toppings and serve warm.

Gingerbread Porridge

Here is a beautiful gingerbread porridge recipe that your kids will love!

Prep Time: 3 minutes

Cook Time: 10 minutes

Servings: 2

Instructions:

Porridge base:

- 2 teaspoons molasses
- ½ cup rolled oats
- 1 teaspoon vanilla extract
- ½ cup almond milk
- ½ cup water
- honey to taste
- 1/8 teaspoon ginger powder

Toppings:

- toasted pecans
- gingerbread biscuits

Directions:

1. Combine all of your oat ingredients in a pot.

2. Bring your oat mixture to a boil over medium heat setting, then reduce to low and simmer for 10-minutes or until the porridge has reached desired consistency.

3. Add your porridge into serving bowls, then add toppings and serve warm.

Vanilla Raspberry Porridge

A porridge recipe that offers a wonderful aroma and tastes so yummy!

Prep Time:3 minutes

Cook Time:10 minutes

Servings:2

Instructions:

Porridge base:

- ½ cup rolled oats
- 1 teaspoon vanilla extract
- ½ cup almond milk
- 2 tablespoons vanilla yogurt
- maple syrup to taste

Toppings:

- toasted cashews
- fresh raspberries or raspberry sauce

Directions:

1. Mix all of your oat ingredients in a pot.

2. Bring your pot to a boil over medium heat setting, then reduce to low heat and simmer for 10-minutes, or until the porridge has reached desired consistency. Stir porridge occasionally throughout the cooking process. Once cooked, remove the pot from heat.

3. Add porridge to serving bowls, then add toppings and serve warm.

Peanut Butter & Jelly Porridge

Delightful peanut butter and jelly porridge recipe that is sure to please the kids!

Prep Time: 3 minutes

Cook Time: 10 minutes

Servings: 2

Instructions:

Porridge base:

- 2 tablespoons peanut butter
- ½ cup rolled oats
- ½ cup water
- 1 teaspoon vanilla extract
- ½ cup almond milk
- honey to taste
- a dash of sea salt

Toppings:

- blackberry jelly or jam
- peanut butter drizzle
- toasted chopped nuts of your choice

Directions:

1. Combine all of your oat ingredients in a pot.

2. Bring the oat mixture to a boil over medium heat setting, then reduce heat to low and simmer for about 10-minutes or till the porridge has reached desired consistency. Stir porridge occasionally during the cooking process. Remove from heat.

3. Add porridge to serving bowls, top with toppings and serve warm.

Pumpkin Pie Porridge

It makes for the perfect fall time porridge recipe that will complement the weather!

Prep Time:3 minutes

Cook Time:10 minutes

Servings:2

Instructions:

Porridge base:

- 2 tablespoons pumpkin puree
- ½ cup rolled oats
- ¼ teaspoon pumpkin pie spice
- ½ cup coconut milk
- ½ cup water
- dash of sea salt
- maple syrup to taste

Toppings:

- toasted pecans
- cinnamon powder
- maple syrup

Directions:

1. Combine all of your ingredients for oats in a pot.

2. Bring the oat mixture to a boil over medium heat setting, then reduce to low and simmer for 10-minutes or until porridge reaches desired consistency. Stir porridge occasionally during the cooking process. Once cooked, remove the pot from heat.

3. Add your porridge to serving bowls, then top with toppings and serve warm.

Middle Eastern Porridge

Enjoy the intense flavours of Middle Eastern porridge in this recipe!

Prep Time: 3 minutes

Cook Time: 10 minutes

Servings: 2

Instructions:

Porridge base:

- 4 dates, pitted and roughly chopped
- ½ cup rolled oats
- 2 teaspoons tahini
- ½ cup almond milk
- ½ cup water
- honey to taste

Toppings:

- raspberry sauce
- sliced figs
- pistachios, chopped

Directions:

1. Combine all of your oat ingredients in a pot.

2. Bring your oat mixture to a boil over medium heat setting, then reduce heat to low and simmer for 10-minutes or until the porridge has reached desired consistency. Stir the porridge occasionally during the cooking process. Once cooked, remove the pot from heat.

3. Add your porridge to your serving bowls, then top with toppings and serve warm.

Banana & Almond Porridge

Here is a wonderful nutrient-packed porridge recipe with almond milk and banana, making the suitable smoothie-like component to this porridge!

Prep Time: 3 minutes

Cook Time: 10 minutes

Servings: 2

Instructions:

Porridge base:

- ½ cup rolled oats
- 1 cup almond milk
- 1 teaspoon vanilla extract
- ½ teaspoon banana extract
- maple syrup to taste

Toppings:

- dark chocolate chips
- roasted almonds, chopped
- sliced fresh bananas

Directions:

1. Combine all of your oat ingredients in a pot.

2. Bring oat mixture to a boil over medium heat setting, then reduce to low and simmer for 10-minutes or until the porridge has reached desired consistency. Occasionally stir the porridge during the cooking process. Once cooked, remove your pot from the heat.

3. Add your porridge to the serving bowls, then top with toppings and serve warm.

Apple Pie Porridge

A porridge recipe that is perfect for serving during the fall season!

Prep Time:3 minutes

Cook Time:10 minutes

Servings:2

Instructions:

Porridge base:

- ¼ teaspoon cinnamon powder
- ½ cup rolled oats
- ½ cup almond milk
- 1 teaspoon vanilla extract
- a dash of nutmeg
- ½ cup water
- brown sugar to taste

Toppings:

- pecans, chopped
- apples, chopped
- maple syrup to taste

Directions:

1. Combine all of ingredients in a pot.

2. Bring your oat ingredients to a boil, then reduce heat to low and simmer for 10-minutes or until the porridge has reached desired consistency. Occasionally stir the porridge during the cooking process. Once cooked, remove the pot from heat.

3. Add your porridge to your serving bowls, then add the toppings and serve warm.

Carrot Cake Porridge

This porridge recipe embodies the essence of the beautiful flavours in carrot cake!

Prep Time: 3 minutes

Cook Time: 10 minutes

Servings: 2

Instructions:

Porridge base:

- 1 carrot, grated
- ½ cup gluten-free rolled oats
- ½ teaspoon ground cinnamon, plus extra for topping
- ¼ teaspoon ground nutmeg
- 2 teaspoons ground flaxseed
- 1 teaspoon vanilla extract
- ½ cup almond milk
- maple syrup to taste
- ½ cup water

Toppings:

- pumpkin seeds
- fresh blueberries and blackberries

Directions:

1. Combine all of your oat ingredients in a pot.

2. Bring the oat mixture to a boil over medium heat setting, then reduce heat to low and simmer for 10-minutes or until desired porridge consistency is reached. Occasionally stir your porridge during the cooking process. Once the porridge is cooked, remove the pot from heat.

3. Add your porridge to serving bowls, then top with toppings and serve warm.

Chocolate Coconut Porridge

A great duo is chocolate and coconut, which is proven in this yummy porridge recipe!

Prep Time: 3 minutes

Cook Time: 10 minutes

Servings: 2

Instructions:

Porridge base:

- ½ cup rolled oats
- 2 teaspoons cocoa powder
- 1 tablespoon desiccated coconut
- 4 dates, pitted and roughly chopped
- 1 teaspoon vanilla extract
- ½ cup almond milk
- ½ cup water
- a dash of sea salt
- maple syrup to taste

Toppings:

- 2 teaspoons cacao nibs
- 1 tablespoon coconut shavings
- maple syrup to taste

Directions:

1. Combine your oat ingredients in a pot.

2. Bring your oat mixture to a boil over medium heat setting, then reduce heat to low and simmer for 10-minutes or until the porridge has reached desired consistency. Occasionally stir porridge during the cooking process. Once cooked, remove the pot from heat.

3. Add your porridge into your serving bowls, then top with toppings and serve warm.

Free Bonus Oatmeal Cookie Recipes

Coconut Oatmeal Cookies

Here is a yummy oatmeal cookie recipe for those that love coconut!

Prep Time: 10 minutes

Cook Time: 12 minutes

Servings: 6 dozen cookies

Instructions:

- 2 cups all-purpose flour
- 1 cup granulated sugar
- 1 cup butter
- 2 cups shredded coconut
- 2 eggs
- 1 teaspoon baking soda
- 2 tablespoons coconut rum
- 1 tablespoon molasses
- 1 teaspoon sea salt
- 2 teaspoons vanilla extract
- 1 teaspoon baking powder
- 1 cup rolled oats

Directions:

1. Cream your butter by slowly adding sugar to the mixing bowl, then beat until light and fluffy.

2. Add the vanilla, eggs while continuing to beat well.

3. Sift together your salt, baking soda, baking powder, and flour.

4. Slowly add your dry ingredients and stir until the oatmeal and coconut flakes.

5. Drop large teaspoonfuls of oat mixture onto an ungreased baking sheet.

6. Bake in preheated oven at 375° Fahrenheit for 15 minutes or until golden. Remove baking sheet and place on a rack to cool.

Peanut Butter, Chocolate Chip, Oatmeal Cookies

The perfect oatmeal recipe, especially for peanut butter and chocolate lovers!

Prep Time: 10 minutes

Cook Time: 12 minutes

Servings: 6 Dozen cookies

Instructions:

- 2 cups all-purpose flour
- 2 cups quick-cooking oats
- ¼ teaspoon sea salt
- 1 teaspoon baking powder
- 1 cup country crock spread
- 1 cup granulated sugar
- 1 cup chunky or creamy peanut butter
- 2 eggs
- 1 cup brown sugar
- 1 (12-ounce) package semi-sweet chocolate chips
- 2 teaspoons vanilla extract

Directions:

1. Preheat your oven to 350° Fahrenheit.

2. In a mixing bowl, mix flour, baking powder, oats, soda, salt, then set aside.

3. In another bowl, using an electric mixer on medium speed, beat your spread and peanut butter until smooth. Beat in your sugars, eggs, and vanilla until well combined.

4. Beat in your flour mixture until well blended. Stir in the chocolate chips.

5. Add rounded tablespoonfuls of cookie mix onto an ungreased baking sheet about 2-inches apart.

6. Bake cookies for about 12-minutes or until golden brown. Remove cookies from the oven and place them on a cooling rack.

Apple & Raisin Oatmeal Cookies

Great and easy-to-prepare apple oatmeal cookie recipe that the kids will love!

Prep Time: 10 minutes

Cook Time: 11 minutes

Servings: 2 dozen

Instructions:

- ¾ cup all-purpose flour
- 1 ½ cups quick-cooking rolled oats
- ½ cup brown sugar
- ¾ cup whole wheat flour
- 1 ½ teaspoons cinnamon
- 1 cup apples, peeled and finely chopped
- ½ teaspoon sea salt
- ½ cup raisins
- 1 egg slightly beaten
- 1/3 cup of milk
- ½ tablespoon oil

Directions:

1. Preheat your oven to 375° Fahrenheit.

2. In a mixing bowl, mix your oats, whole wheat flour, all-purpose flour, brown sugar, baking powder, baking soda, sea salt, and cinnamon, then stir to combine.

3. Stir in the apples and raisins.

4. In a large mixing bowl, mix egg, honey, milk and oil. Stir in the dry ingredients and mix to form a smooth batter.

5. Drop the batter by the tablespoonfuls onto ungreased baking sheets, leaving 2-inches apart.

6. Bake cookies for 12 minutes or until lightly golden.

7. Remove your cookies from the oven, then place them on a cooling rack.

Currant Spice Oatmeal Cookies

Here is a yummy and spicy tasting oatmeal cookie recipe that is sure to please!

Prep Time: 10 minutes

Cook Time: 12 minutes

Servings: 30 cookies

Instructions:

- 1 ½ teaspoons vanilla extract
- 2 large eggs
- 2/3 cup dried currants
- 1 teaspoon baking soda
- ¾ teaspoon sea salt
- ½ teaspoon ground cinnamon
- 1 2/3 cups all-purpose flour
- ¾ teaspoon ground cardamom
- ¼ teaspoon ground allspice
- 1 cup brown sugar
- 1 cup unsalted butter
- 2 cups old-fashioned oats

Directions:

1. First, preheat your oven to 350° Fahrenheit.

2. In a mixer, combine the sugar and butter until smooth.

3. Add baking soda, vanilla, spices, and salt. Blend well.

4. Blend in your currants, oats, then the flour.

5. Roll the batter in the palms of your hands into a tablespoon size ball and place it onto an ungreased cookie sheet.

6. Bake cookies for 12 minutes in batches. Place baked cookies on cooling racks.

Chewy Walnut Oatmeal Cookies

If you enjoy chewy cookies and have nuts in them, then give this recipe a try!

Prep Time: 10 minutes

Cook Time: 10 minutes

Servings: 2 dozen

Instructions:

- 1 cup brown sugar
- 1 cup white sugar
- 2 eggs
- 1 cup butter
- 3 cups quick oatmeal
- 2 cups flour
- 1 teaspoon baking soda
- 1 cup chocolate chips
- 1 teaspoon vanilla extract
- ½ teaspoon sea salt
- 1 cup walnuts, finely chopped
- 1 cup raisins

Directions:

1. Beat your butter and sugar with a mixer on medium speed.

2. Beat your eggs and add vanilla.

3. Combine cookie mix, then add tablespoonfuls of mix to ungreased cookie sheets about 2-inches apart. Bake for 10-minutes or until golden brown. Set on a rack to cool.

Conclusion

I truly hope that you and those close to you, enjoy my collection of porridge recipes as much as my loved ones and I do! Make your morning meal more exciting by trying new and different toppings to your porridge. Trying new dishes will help to liven things up and get your day off to a good start! Use my collection of porridge recipes as a guide into the beautiful world of porridge and' many flavours that it offers! I always encourage people to try and use my recipes as a base. Adding their ingredients into the recipe suits their tastes—thus truly making and creating their unique recipes! Not only is this collection of recipes flavourful and yummy, but they are highly nutritious as well. Any time I can combine healthy and tasty in the same recipe, that is what I call a "win-win" for sure! Nothing tastes better than a flavourful meal with the knowledge that it is not only pleasing your taste buds but is also a healthy choice in foods! These porridge recipes are very simple and easy to prepare, so you can be sitting down to enjoy your warm bowl of porridge within minutes!

About the Author

Nancy Silverman is an accomplished chef from Essex, Vermont. Armed with her degree in Nutrition and Food Sciences from the University of Vermont, Nancy has excelled at creating e-books that contain healthy and delicious meals that anyone can make and everyone can enjoy. She improved her cooking skills at the New England Culinary Institute in Montpelier Vermont and she has been working at perfecting her culinary style since graduation. She claims that her life's work is always a work in progress and she only hopes to be an inspiration to aspiring chefs everywhere.

Her greatest joy is cooking in her modern kitchen with her family and creating inspiring and delicious meals. She often says that she has perfected her signature dishes based on her family's critique of each and every one.

Nancy has her own catering company and has also been fortunate enough to be head chef at some of Vermont's most exclusive restaurants. When a friend suggested she share some of her outstanding signature dishes, she decided to add cookbook author to her repertoire of personal achievements. Being a technological savvy woman, she felt the e-book realm would be a better fit and soon she had her first cookbook available online. As of today, Nancy has sold over 1,000 e-books and has shared her culinary experiences and brilliant recipes with people from all over the world! She plans on expanding into self-help books and dietary cookbooks, so stayed tuned!

Author's Afterthoughts

Thank you for making the decision to invest in one of my cookbooks! I cherish all my readers and hope you find joy in preparing these meals as I have.

There are so many books available and I am truly grateful that you decided to buy this one and follow it from beginning to end.

I love hearing from my readers on what they thought of this book and any value they received from reading it. As a personal favor, I would appreciate any feedback you can give in the form of a review on Amazon and please be honest! This kind of support will help others make an informed choice on and will help me tremendously in producing the best quality books possible.

My most heartfelt thanks,

Nancy Silverman

If you're interested in more of my books, be sure to follow my author page on Amazon (can be found on the link Bellow) or scan the QR-Code.

https://www.amazon.com/author/nancy-silverman

Printed in Great Britain
by Amazon

20416505R00047